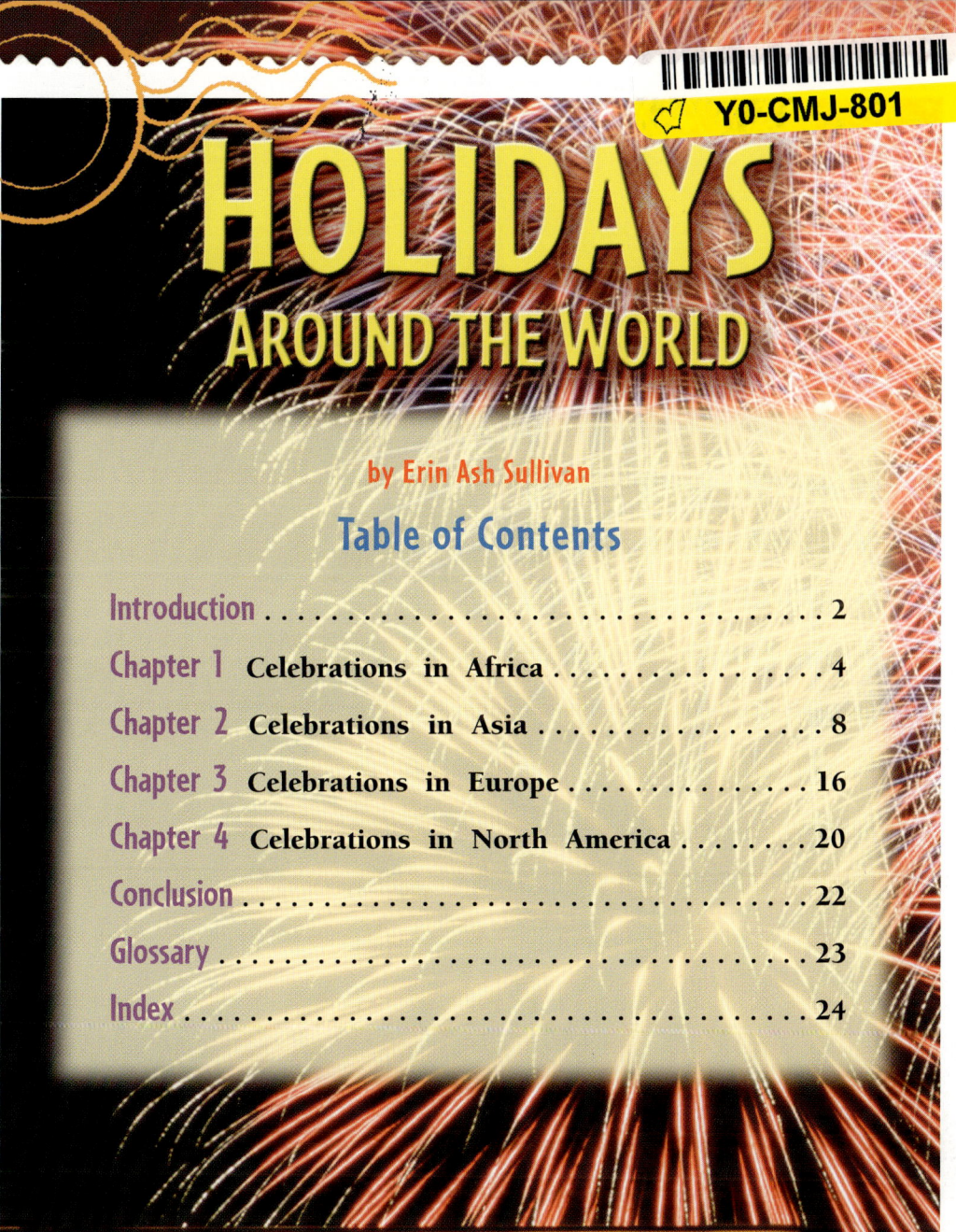

HOLIDAYS AROUND THE WORLD

by Erin Ash Sullivan

Table of Contents

Introduction	2
Chapter 1 Celebrations in Africa	4
Chapter 2 Celebrations in Asia	8
Chapter 3 Celebrations in Europe	16
Chapter 4 Celebrations in North America	20
Conclusion	22
Glossary	23
Index	24

Introduction

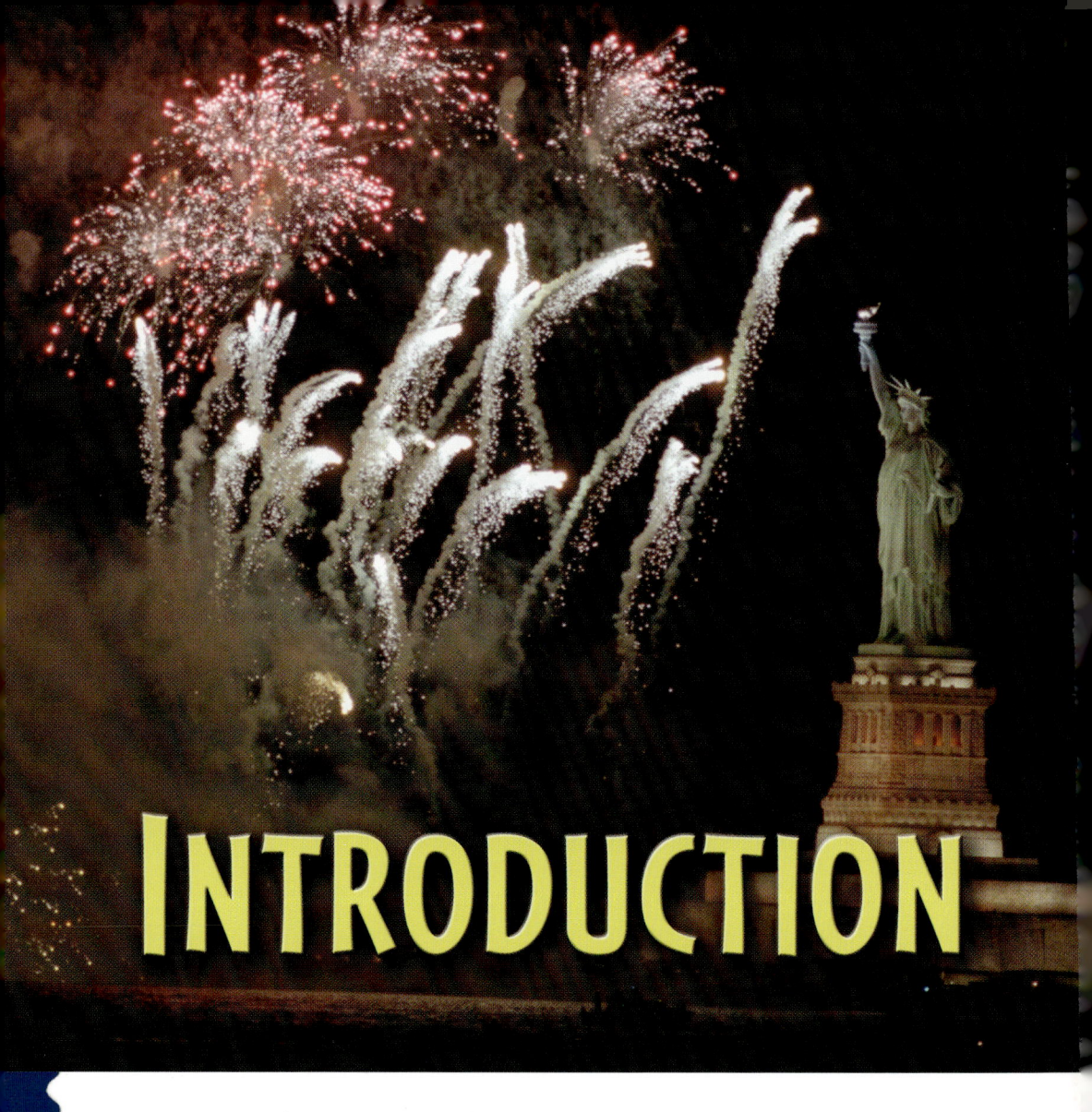

What are your favorite days of the year? Some of them might be **holidays**. Holidays are special days that people **celebrate**. People have a good time on holidays.

Why do people have holidays? Sometimes people honor special times in the history of their country. Sometimes people celebrate a change in the seasons.

Why do people enjoy celebrations? They are an exciting change from daily life. People get together. Sometimes they have parties. There might be music and dancing, and there is good food to eat.

In this book, you'll read about different holidays around the world. You'll also learn about different **traditions** (truh-DIH-shuhnz). Traditions are special ways of celebrating that have been passed down through the years.

You'll also see that there is one thing that all celebrations have in common: they're fun!

▲ In Mexico, people celebrate Cinco de Mayo. It is an important holiday.

CHAPTER 1

CELEBRATIONS IN AFRICA

NIGERIA: Fishing Festival

Some people think it's hard to catch fish with a fishing pole. Now imagine trying to catch a fish with only a net and a hollowed-out **gourd**—a round fruit, like a squash or a pumpkin.

▲ Nigeria lies on the western coast of Africa.

▲ The fishing contest is short. It's over in just one hour!

That's what happens every February at the Argungu Fishing Festival in Nigeria, where people come to celebrate the **harvest**. Hundreds of men gather for a fishing contest. They line up along the riverbank. Then the contest starts. The men dash into the water. They use their nets to catch the fish. They use the gourds to hold the fish after they have been caught.

Imagine the excitement. Boats carry drummers beating their drums. Other men rattle gourds filled with seeds. They believe the noise will make the fish move to shallow water.

Who wins the contest? It is the person who catches the biggest fish!

Math Matters

At one fishing festival, it took four men to lift the winning fish onto the scale. It weighed 165 pounds (75 kilograms). That's about the weight of a grown man!

CHAPTER 1

GHANA: Yam Festival

What kind of food do you eat most often? If you lived in Ghana, you would eat lots of yams. A yam is a sweet, starchy vegetable that looks a little like a potato. It's one of the most important foods in Ghana.

Every year, the people of Ghana celebrate the yam harvest with a big festival. The festival is full of traditions that are hundreds of years old.

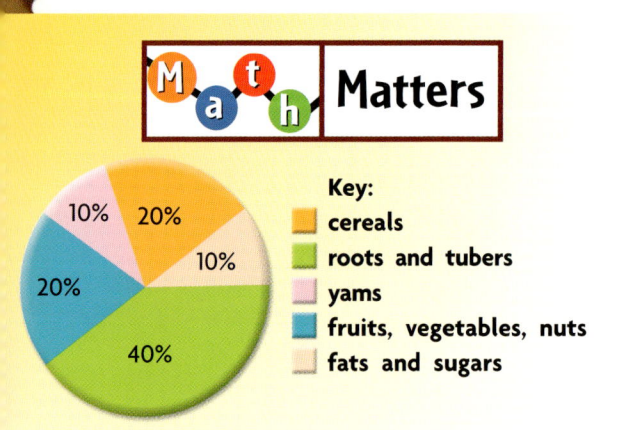

▲ Ghana is on the western coast of Africa.

Math Matters

Key:
- cereals
- roots and tubers
- yams
- fruits, vegetables, nuts
- fats and sugars

10%, 20%, 10%, 20%, 40%

This graph shows the kinds of foods that people usually eat in Ghana. How is this similar to what you eat every day? How is it different?

▼ Like potatoes, yams grow under the ground.

6

CELEBRATIONS IN AFRICA

Before the festival, people in each village go to the river to wash special stools. The stools honor **ancestors** (AN-sehs-tuhrz), people in a family who have died. People use the stools to remember their ancestors and show respect to their family. Then people clean their homes. They also close the roads to the village to keep bad spirits away.

Some villagers carefully dig up the new yams. They bring the yams to the chief, who blesses them. After this happens, the festival can begin!

People start to cook. Delicious smells float through the village.

▲ In Ghana, stools are more than just places to sit. They are special pieces of furniture that are used in celebrations.

That night, everyone feasts. There is drumming and dancing. People are thankful that there is plenty of food and that the harvest has gone well.

CHAPTER 2

CELEBRATIONS IN ASIA

CHINA: Chinese New Year

It is February. Noise from music and fireworks fills the air. The smell of food cooking fills your nose. Everywhere you look, you can see the color red. What holiday is this? It's the Chinese New Year.

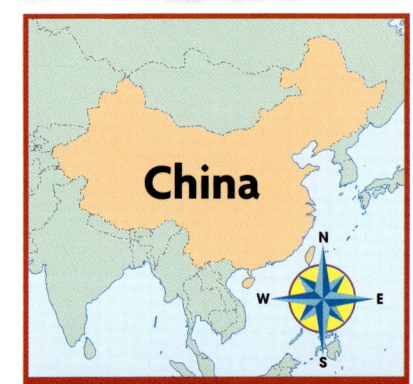

▲ More people live in China than in any other country in the world.

▲ One of the best parts of Chinese New Year is the dragon parade. The dragon is a **symbol** of strength and good luck.

Math Matters

Some dragon puppets can be up to 100 feet (30.5 meters) long. That's longer than two school buses!

Chinese people think of the New Year as a new beginning. They clean their houses. They give their doors and windows a fresh coat of red paint. People believe that the color red brings good luck. Red stands for strength and energy. Parents give their children red envelopes with money inside for good luck.

The night before the New Year, families eat a special meal. They eat dried oysters, seaweed, and dumplings. At midnight, there are fireworks.

It's a Fact

Chinese New Year is on a different day in January or February every year. That's because the Chinese calendar is different from the one used in the U.S. and Canada.

Chinese New Year is a fun celebration. It is a time when people plan for the future. How is this like your own New Year's celebration?

CHAPTER 2

JAPAN: Girl's Day and Boy's Day

Sometimes it's fun to celebrate just being you. In Japan, people celebrate the girls and boys in their families with Girl's Day and Boy's Day. These celebrations have been around for hundreds of years. It's one way for Japanese people to be thankful that their children are happy and healthy.

▲ Japan is a small island nation off the coast of Asia.

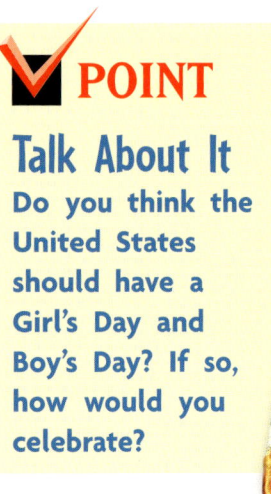

✓POINT

Talk About It
Do you think the United States should have a Girl's Day and Boy's Day? If so, how would you celebrate?

a Girl's Day doll ▶

CELEBRATIONS IN ASIA

Girl's Day is on March 3rd. This day is also called the Doll Festival. Every family has a special set of dolls dressed in old Japanese costumes. These dolls are passed down from mother to daughter.

On Girl's Day, families put the dolls in a **shrine**. A shrine is a place where people put special objects. Each of the dolls goes in a special place in the shrine.

▲ Every Girl's Day doll has a special place in the shrine.

Girl's Day is a day full of food and parties. There are parties at school. Families get together. People eat diamond-shaped rice cakes.

As soon as Girl's Day is over, families take down the doll shrine. They believe it is bad luck to leave the dolls out after March 3rd.

CHAPTER 2

Boy's Day is on May 5th. People put out small model soldiers. Often, the models are very old. They have been passed down from father to son over the years. Families also put out small models of old weapons and **armor**. Armor is the special covering worn by soldiers for protection.

▲ A carp is a kind of fish. On Boy's Day, every family puts up a special bamboo pole with paper carp attached like flags. There is one carp for each boy in the family.

CELEBRATIONS IN ASIA

There is also special food to eat on Boy's Day. There are dumplings and rice cakes with sweet bean paste. These foods are eaten every year on Boy's Day.

Children in Japan look forward to Girl's Day and Boy's Day each year. What a great way to make girls and boys feel special!

It's a Fact

There's another Japanese holiday for children called "Seven-Five-Three." It celebrates children who are seven, five, and three years old. Japanese people believe that odd numbers, like seven, five, and three, are lucky. On this holiday, it is a tradition for children to get three long candies in a bag.

◀ One of the most popular Boy's Day soldiers is Kintaro. He was a Japanese boy who grew up to become a general.

CHAPTER 2

INDIA: Holi

You wake up one morning and look out your window. You see a group of children covered in paint. What's going on? If you lived in India, you would know that people are celebrating Holi (HOH-lee).

Holi celebrates the wheat harvest. The harvest is the time when crops are ripe and ready to be picked. In India, Holi is a time for games, parties, jokes, and fun.

▲ India is a peninsula (puh-NIHN-suh-luh). A peninsula is a piece of land that is surrounded by water on three sides.

Historical Perspective

The tradition of throwing paint powder, or gulal (goo-LAHL), comes from very old stories about an Indian god named Krishna. Krishna liked to play jokes on people, and he liked to throw colored water on his friends. Today, people remember those ancient stories by throwing gulal at each other on Holi.

CELEBRATIONS IN ASIA

▲ After everyone gets covered with paint, it's time to clean up. People put on fresh clothes and visit friends.

On Holi, people build piles of wood. Then they light the wood to make huge **bonfires**. People gather around the bonfires. They laugh and tell stories.

For children, the best part of Holi is the paint. Children cover each other with different colors of paint powder called gulal. Then they squirt colored water at each other! They use hoses, buckets, and even water guns. It's like a huge water fight. By the end, everyone is wet and covered in a rainbow of colors.

Holi is a day to celebrate friendships and have fun. But watch out for that paint!

CHAPTER 3

CELEBRATIONS IN EUROPE

SWEDEN: St. Lucia's Day

If you're a child living in Sweden, you probably wake up early on December 13th. It's the Festival of St. Lucia, and you have an important job to do.

On St. Lucia's Day, the oldest girl in the house puts on a beautiful white dress. She ties a red sash around her waist. Then she puts a **wreath**—a circle of leaves—on her head. The wreath has battery-powered candles on top. Boys put on special outfits, too. They wear white robes and special hats decorated with stars.

▲ Dressed in their white dresses and red sashes, these girls are performing St. Lucia's Day and Christmas songs.

16

Then it's off to the kitchen. The children bring their parents breakfast in bed! What's to eat? It's a special St. Lucia's cake, called *lussekatt* (LOO-suh-kaht). It's shaped like an "S." The children serve the *lussekatt* with hot coffee. Sometimes there are ginger cookies, too. As the children serve the food, they sing special songs for St. Lucia's Day.

▲ *Lussekatt* is a special cake served on St. Lucia's Day.

Children also bring *lussekatt* to their teachers at school. Many towns have St. Lucia's Day parades. The children wear their special outfits. People get together to share meals and enjoy the winter season.

Historical Perspective

St. Lucia's Day is a way to celebrate light during the dark days of winter. Long ago, people celebrated with candles. Today, they use electric lights.

CHAPTER 3

ENGLAND: May Day

May Day is May 1st. After the long winter, people in England look forward to spring. The weather is warmer. Plants and flowers grow again. It's a good time to celebrate the change in the seasons.

▲ England is an island country.

Many villages celebrate May Day with a big festival. The people choose a girl to be the May Queen. People play games and hold contests.

▲ Maypole dancing is one tradition of the May Day celebration. These children are performing at Leeds Castle in England.

CELEBRATIONS IN EUROPE

A favorite part of May Day is the **maypole**. It's a tall, thin pole with long ribbons that hang down from the top. People gather around the maypole. Each person takes the end of one of the ribbons. As the people walk around the maypole, the ribbons make a beautiful pattern. Long ago, the maypole dance was a symbol for the change of the seasons. Today, it's a fun tradition that everyone enjoys.

Another part of the May Day celebration is Morris dancing. Morris dancing has been a tradition in England for hundreds of years. Sometimes Morris dancers wear special shoes called clogs. Sometimes they use sticks and handkerchiefs as part of their dance.

▲ Morris dancers also dance with swords. Many years ago, the sword dances may have helped the dancers practice for battle.

CHAPTER 4

CELEBRATIONS IN NORTH AMERICA

MEXICO: Cinco de Mayo

Mexico is a fun place to be on May 5th. It's Cinco de Mayo (SIHNK-oh duh MY-oh). *Cinco de Mayo* means "the fifth of May" in Spanish.

▲ Mexico is just south of the United States.

On this day, Mexicans remember a famous battle that happened in 1862. The French army tried to invade Mexico. The Mexicans fought back and won the battle.

▲ These girls are marching in a Cinco de Mayo parade in Puebla, Mexico.

In Mexico, Cinco de Mayo is a day to celebrate Mexican independence. It's also a day to celebrate Mexican culture.

Many towns have Cinco de Mayo parades. People dress up in special clothes and play Mexican music. Everywhere you look, you can see the colors of the Mexican flag: green, white, and red.

▲ Children look forward to hitting the piñata during Cinco de Mayo.

✓ POINT Picture It

Reread this page. Draw a picture of some of the things you might see on Cinco de Mayo.

People have Cinco de Mayo parties. They eat delicious traditional foods, such as tortillas. Tortillas are thin, round cakes made of corn or flour. There are also tamales, which are made of meat or vegetables wrapped in dough and then boiled in a cornhusk. Many foods are flavored with spicy red peppers.

Cinco de Mayo is also celebrated in many parts of the United States. It's a reminder that people in different parts of the world share traditions.

CONCLUSION

Around the world, people enjoy holidays and celebrations. We look forward to getting together with friends and family. We enjoy going to parties and eating delicious foods. Year after year, every country celebrates its own special traditions. When you learn about a country's holidays, you also learn about the people who live there.

This chart lists all the holidays that you have read about in this book. Take a closer look. How are some of these holidays the same? How are they different?

Country	Holiday	What It Celebrates
Nigeria	Fishing Festival	harvest
Ghana	Yam Festival	yam harvest
China	Chinese New Year	the change in seasons
Japan	Boy's and Girl's Days	children
India	Holi	wheat harvest
Sweden	St. Lucia's Day	the winter season
England	May Day	the coming of spring
Mexico	Cinco de Mayo	Mexican independence and culture

GLOSSARY

ancestor (AN-sehs-tuhr) a person from whom one is descended (page 7)

armor (AHR-muhr) special covering worn by soldiers long ago for protection (page 12)

bonfire (BAHN-fyr) a large fire built outdoors (page 15)

celebrate (SEHL-uh-brayt) to honor a special day or event with ceremonies and other activities (page 2)

gourd (GORD) a rounded fruit related to the pumpkin or squash (page 4)

harvest (HAHR-vihst) the gathering in of a crop when it is ripe (page 5)

holiday (HAH-lih-day) a special day when people get together for fun (page 2)

maypole (MAY-pohl) a tall pole with long ribbons used during May Day (page 19)

shrine (SHRYN) a table or shelf where people put special holiday objects (page 11)

symbol (SIHM-buhl) an object that stands for an idea (page 8)

tradition (truh-DIH-shuhn) a special way of celebrating that happens over and over again (page 3)

wreath (REETH) a circle of leaves and branches used for decoration (page 16)

INDEX

ancestor, 7
armor, 12
bonfire, 15
Boy's Day, 10, 12–13
celebrate, 2, 5–6, 10, 14–15, 18, 21–22
China, 8–9
Chinese New Year, 8–9
Cinco de Mayo, 20–21
England, 18–19
Fishing Festival, 4–5
Ghana, 6–7
Girl's Day, 10–11, 13
gourd, 4–5
gulal, 15
harvest, 5–7, 14
Holi, 14–15
holiday, 2–3, 8, 22
India, 14–15
Japan, 10–13
lussekatt, 17
May Day, 18–19
maypole, 19
Mexico, 20–21
Morris dancers, 19
Nigeria, 4–5
St. Lucia's Day, 16–17
shrine, 11
Sweden, 16–17
symbol, 8, 19
tradition, 3, 6, 19, 21–22
wreath, 16
Yam Festival, 6–7

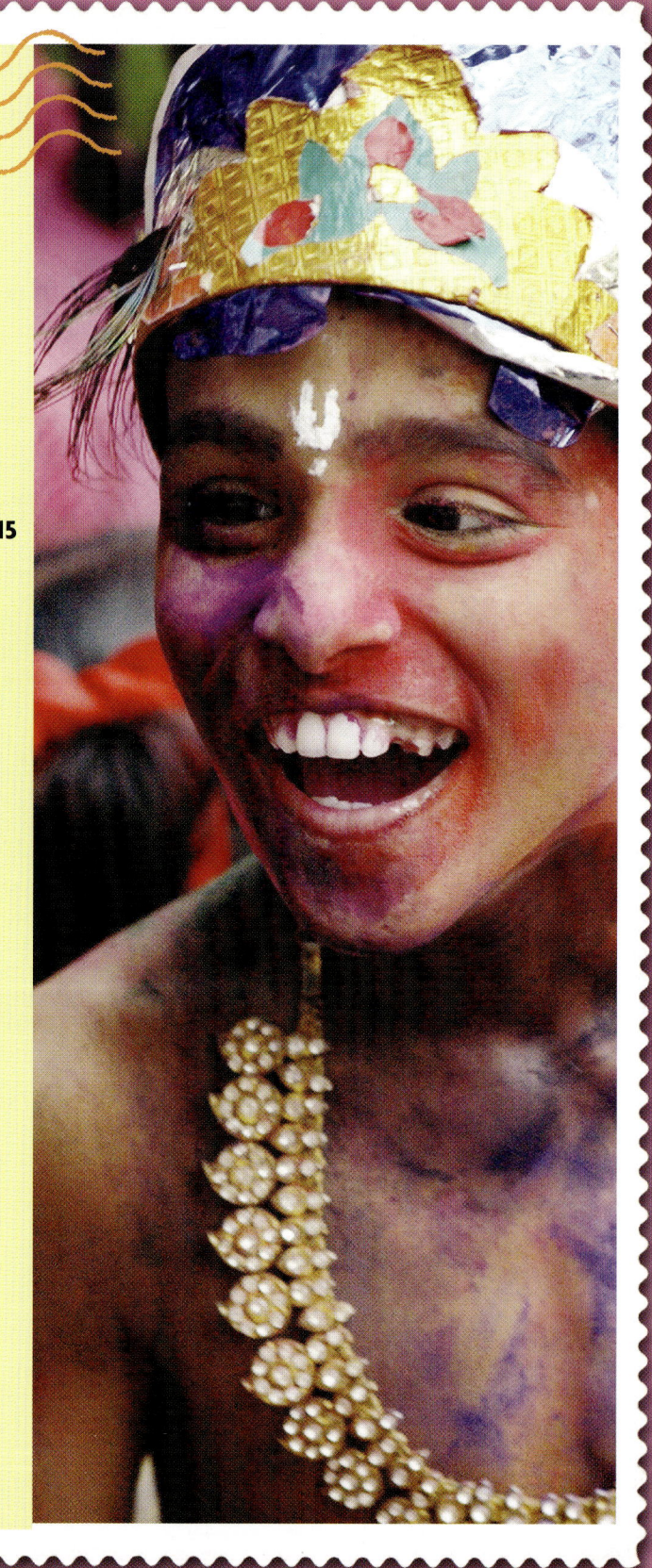